SEPARATION AND SERVICE

OR, THOUGHTS ON NUMBERS VI, VII

J. HUDSON TAYLOR

This edition first published 2025
by Cosmic Jive Publishing

978-1-918219-42-5

INTRODUCTORY

FOR MANY YEARS these chapters had no special interest to me; but I have never ceased to be thankful that I was early led to read the Word of GOD in regular course: it was through this habit that these chapters first became specially precious to me. I was travelling on a missionary tour in the province of CHEH-KIANG, and had to pass the night in a very wicked town. All the inns were dreadful places; and the people seemed to have their consciences seared, and their hearts sealed against the Truth. My own heart was oppressed, and could find no relief; and I awoke the next morning much cast down, and feeling spiritually hungry and thirsty indeed.

On opening my Bible at the seventh chapter of Numbers, I felt as though I could not then read that long chapter of repetitions; that I *must* turn to some chapter that would feed my soul. And yet I was not happy in leaving my regular portion; so after a little conflict I resolved to read it, praying to GOD to bless me, even through Numb. vii. I fear there was not much faith in the prayer; but oh! how abundantly it was answered, and what a feast GOD gave me! He revealed to me His own great heart of love, and gave me the key to understand this and the previous chapter as never before. May GOD make our meditations upon them as helpful to others as they were then and have ever since continued to be to myself.

Much is revealed in these chapters in germ which is more fully brought out in the New Testament. Under the Old Covenant many blessings were enjoyed in measure and for a season, which in this dispensation are ours in their fulness and permanence. For instance, the atoning sacrifices of the seventh month had to be repeated every year; but CHRIST, in offering Himself once for all, perfected for ever them that are sanctified. The Psalmist needed to pray, "Take not Thy HOLY SPIRIT from me;" but CHRIST has

Separation and Service

given us the COMFORTER to abide with us for ever. In like manner the Israelite might vow the vow of a Nazarite and separate himself unto GOD for a season; but it is the privilege of the Christian believer to know himself as always separated to GOD. Many other lessons, which are hidden from careless and superficial readers, are suggested by these chapters, which the HOLY SPIRIT will reveal to prayerful students of His most precious and most perfect Book.

The portions we have selected consist of first a short chapter, and then a very long one, which at first sight appears to have no special connection with it. But on more careful reflection we shall see that the order of the subjects referred to shows that there is really a natural and close connection between them. We shall find that Separation to GOD is followed by Blessing from GOD; and that those who receive large blessing from Him, in turn render to Him acceptable Service: service in which GOD takes delight, and which He places in everlasting remembrance.

PART I
Separation to God

Numb. vi. 1-21

THE INSTITUTION OF THE ORDER OF NAZARITES

THE FIRST TWENTY-ONE verses of Numb. vi. give us an account of the institution and ordinances of the order of Nazarites. And let us note at the outset that this institution, like every other good and perfect gift, came from above; that God Himself gave this privilege—unasked—to His people; thereby showing His desire that "whosoever will" of His people may be brought into closest relationship to Himself.

It was very gracious of GOD to *permit* His people to become Nazarites. Israel might have been "a kingdom of priests;" but through their own sin they had nationally forfeited this privilege, and a special family had been set apart to the priesthood. GOD, however, still opened the way for individuals who wished to draw near to Him to do so, and for any period which their own hearts might dictate.

But it is important to notice that though the vow might only be one of temporary consecration, yet it involved while it lasted an

ABSOLUTE ACCEPTANCE

of the will of GOD, even in regard to matters which might appear trivial and unimportant. So, in the present day, GOD is willing to give to His people fulness of blessing, but it must be on His own lines. Though we are not our own, it is, alas! possible to live as though we were; devotion to GOD is still a voluntary thing; hence the differences of attainment among Christians. While salvation is a free gift, the "winning CHRIST" can only be through unreserved consecration and unquestioning obedience. Nor is this a hardship, but the highest privilege.

Let us now look into the law of the Nazarite.

IMPLICIT OBEDIENCE: verses 3, 4.

"He shall separate himself from wine and strong drink, and shall drink no vinegar of wine, or vinegar of strong drink, neither shall he drink any liquor of grapes, nor eat moist grapes, or dried. All the days of his separation shall he eat nothing that is made of the vine tree, from the kernels even to the husk."

The first thing that we note is, that as the obedience of Adam was tested in the Garden by the prohibition of one tree—a tree pleasant to look upon, and good for food—so was the obedience of the Nazarite tested. He was not forbidden to eat poison berries, nor was he merely required to abstain from the wine and strong drink which might easily become a snare; fresh grapes and dried raisins were equally prohibited. It was not that the thing was harmful in itself, but that the doing the will of GOD, in a matter of seeming indifference, was essential to his acceptance.

Not less true is this of the Christian Nazarite. Whether he eat or drink, or whatsoever he do, the will of GOD and not self-indulgence must be his one aim. Christians often get into perplexity about worldly allurements by asking, Where is the sin of this, or the danger of that? There *may* be danger that the questioner cannot see: Satan's baits often skilfully conceal a sharp hook; but supposing that the thing be harmless, it does not follow that it would be pleasing to GOD, or spiritually helpful.

The fruit of the vine is a type of earth-born pleasures; those who would enjoy Nazarite nearness to GOD must count His love "better than wine." To win CHRIST, the Apostle Paul gladly suffered the loss of all things, and counted them as dross and dung for the excellency of the knowledge of CHRIST JESUS his LORD. The things he gave up were not bad things, but good—

things that in themselves were gain to him; and CHRIST Himself for our redemption emptied Himself, and came to seek not His own, but the will of Him that sent Him.

The highest service demands the greatest sacrifice, but it secures the fullest blessing and the greatest fruitfulness. CHRIST could not remain in His FATHER'S bosom and redeem the world; missionaries cannot win the heathen and enjoy their home surroundings; nor can they be adequately sustained without the loving sacrifices of many friends and donors. You, dear reader, know th MASTER'S choice; what is YOURS? is it to do His will even if it mean to leave all for Him, to give all to Him?

ENTIRE CONSECRATION: verse 5.

"All the days of the vow of his separation there shall no razor come upon his head: until the days be fulfilled, in the which he separateth himself unto the LORD, he shall be holy, and shall let the locks of the hair of his head grow."

We have already seen that GOD tested the obedience of the Nazarite in the matter of food: pleasing GOD was rather to be chosen than the most tempting cluster of grapes. But in the foregoing words we find that his obedience is further tested, and this in a way which to many might prove a more severe trial. GOD claims the right of determining the personal appearance of His servant, and directs that separated ones should be manifestly such. To many minds there is the greatest shrinking from appearing peculiar; but GOD would often have His people unmistakably peculiar. We sometimes hear the argument, "all the world" thinks this, or does that, given as a reason for our doing likewise; but that is an argument that should have no weight with the Christian, who is commanded *not* to be conformed to the world. While we are not to seek to be peculiar for its own sake, we are not to hesitate to be so when duty to GOD renders it necessary, or when the privilege of self-denial for the benefit of others calls for it.

Further, this command again reminded

Separation and Service

the Nazarite that he was not his own, but was utterly the LORD'S; that GOD claimed the very hair of his head. He was not at liberty to cut or trim it as he saw fit, nor to wear it as long or as short as might be agreeable to himself. So absolute was GOD'S claim upon him, that not merely while his vow lasted was that hair to be recognised as GOD'S possession, but when his vow was fulfilled the whole of it was to be shaved off, and was to be burnt upon the altar. Like the burnt-offering, it was to be recognised as for GOD'S use alone, whether or not any utilitarian purpose were accomplished by the sacrifice.

So now, in the present dispensation, we are told "the very hairs of your head are all numbered"—so minute is GOD'S care for His people, so watchful is He over all that affects them. It is beautiful to see the fond love of a young mother as she passes her fingers through the silken locks of her darling child—her treasure and her delight; *but she never counts those hairs.* He only, who is the source of mother-love, does that! And shall not *we*, who are not our own, but bought with a price, *gladly* render to Him *all* we are and have—every member of our body, every fibre of our being, every faculty of our mind, all our will-power, and all our love?

HOLINESS TO THE LORD: verses 6-8.

"All the days that he separateth himself unto the LORD he shall come at no dead body. He shall not make himself unclean for his father, or for his mother, for his brother, or for his sister, when they die; because the consecration of his GOD is upon his head. All the days of his separation he is holy unto the LORD."

Here we have a most solemn and important prohibition—to refrain from all uncleanness caused by contact with death. Death is the wages of sin: the consecrated one was alike to keep aloof from sin and from its consequences.

No requirement of GOD'S Word is more clear than the command to honour and obey our earthly parents; but even for his father or mother a Nazarite might not *defile* himself: "he that loveth father or mother more than ME, is not worthy of ME."

But let no young Christian think lightly of the requirements of parents, when these do *not* conflict with GOD'S written Word. Young Christians are sometimes distressed because their desire to preach the Gospel to the heathen has been opposed by parents: such should be encouraged to *thank* GOD for the obstacle; and to seek by prayer its removal. When they have learnt to move man through GOD at home, they will be the better prepared to do the same thing in the mission-field. Where there is fitness for the work, the way will probably be made plain after a time of patient waiting.

These verses teach us that mere contact with death is defiling: how vain then is the imagination of the unconverted that by dead works—the best efforts of those who are themselves dead in trespasses and sins—they can render themselves acceptable to GOD! The good works of the unsaved may indeed benefit their fellow-creatures; but until life in CHRIST has been received, they cannot please GOD.

UNWITTING DEFILEMENT: verses 9-12.

"If any man die very suddenly by him, and he hath defiled the head of his consecration; then he shall shave his head in the day of his cleansing, on the seventh day shall he shave it. And on the eighth day he shall bring two turtles, or two young pigeons, to the priest, to the door of the tabernacle of the congregation: and the priest shall offer the one for a sin-offering, and the other for a burnt-offering, and make an atonement for him, for that he sinned by the dead, and shall hallow his head that same day. And he shall consecrate unto the LORD the days of his separation, and shall bring a lamb of the first year for a trespass-offering: but the days that were before shall be lost, because his separation was defiled."

A most important truth is here taught —that even unwitting contact with death might bring sin upon the Nazarite. Sometimes we are tempted to excuse

Separation and Service

ourselves, and to forget the absolute sinfulness of sin, apart altogether from the question of premeditation, or even of consciousness, *at the time*, on our part. The one who became defiled, *was defiled*, whether intentionally or not; GOD'S requirement was absolute, and where not fulfilled the vow was broken; the sin-offering had to be offered, and the service recommenced.

THE HEINOUSNESS OF SIN.

The teaching here, and that of offerings for sins of ignorance, is much needed in this day, when there is a dangerous tendency in some quarters to regard sin as misfortune, and not as guilt. The awful *character* of sin is shown to mankind by its *consequences*. Man's heart is so darkened by the Fall, and by personal sinfulness, that otherwise he would regard sin as a very small matter. But when we think of all the pain that men and women have endured since the Creation, of all the miseries of which this world has been witness, of all the sufferings of the animal creation, and of the eternal as well as temporal consequences of sin, we must see that that which has brought such a harvest of misery into the world is far more awful than sin-blinded men have thought it to be.

The highest evidence, however, of the terrible character of sin is to be found at the Cross; that it needed such a sacrifice —the sacrifice of the SON of GOD—to bring in atonement and everlasting salvation, is surely the most convincing proof of its heinous character.

Death was brought into the world by sin; and, like all the other consequences of sin, it is loathsome and defiling. Man seeks to adorn death; the pageantry of the funeral, the attractiveness of the cemetery, all show this. The Egyptian sought in vain to make the mortal body incorruptible by embalming it. But we have to bury our dead out of our sight, and the believer is taught to look forward to the resurrection.

CLEANSING ONLY THROUGH SACRIFICE.

Let us not lose sight of the fact that the accidental death of any one near the Nazarite—that the thoughtless putting forth of the hand even—might violate his vow of consecration as truly, if not as guiltily, as an act of deliberate transgression; in either case all the previous time was lost, and the period of consecration had to be recommenced after his cleansing. And that cleansing could only be brought about through sacrifice; the sin-offering must *die*; the burnt-offering must *die*; without shedding of blood there could be no remission. So serious was the effect of transgression—and yet, thank GOD, it was not irremediable.

The bearing of this on the life of consecration to GOD in the present day is important. Nearness to GOD calls for tenderness of conscience, thoughtfulness in service, and implicit obedience. If we become conscious of the slightest failure, even through inadvertence, let us not excuse it, but at once humble ourselves before GOD, and confess it, seeking forgiveness and cleansing on the ground of the accepted sacrifice of CHRIST. GOD'S Word is, "If we confess our sins, He is faithful and just to forgive us our sins, and *to cleanse us* from all unrighteousness." This cleansing must be accepted by faith, and a walk "in the light" be at once resumed. And shall we not reverently ask and trust the HOLY SPIRIT to guard and keep us from inadvertence, and to bring to our remembrance those things which we may be in danger of forgetting?

ACCEPTANCE ONLY IN CHRIST:
verses 13-15.

"And this is the law of the Nazarite, when the days of his separation are fulfilled: he shall be brought unto the door of the tabernacle of the congregation; And he shall offer his offering unto the LORD, one he-lamb of the first year without blemish for a burnt-offering, and one ewe-lamb of the first year without blemish for a

sin-offering, and one ram without blemish for peace-offerings, and a basket of unleavened bread, cakes of fine flour mingled with oil, and wafers of unleavened bread anointed with oil, and their meat-offering, and their drink-offerings."

Having seen the character of the vow of the Nazarite, and of the ordinances to be observed should the vow be violated, the case of a Nazarite who has duly fulfilled his vow is next dealt with. He has carried out all GOD'S requirements, and his conscience is void of offence: before GOD and man he is blameless. May he not now congratulate himself, and claim some measure of merit, seeing he has rendered to GOD an acceptable service, and among men has borne a consistent testimony? The offerings to be made on the conclusion of his vow give an impressive answer to this question, and bring out the important difference between being *blameless* and being *sinless*. Having fulfilled the ordinances he was blameless; but the necessity alike for sin-offering, for burnt-offering, and for peace offering, remind us of the sin of our holy things;

and that not our worst, but our best, is only acceptable to GOD through the atonement of our LORD JESUS CHRIST.

While, however, the best services of the believer can neither give full satisfaction to his own enlightened conscience, nor be acceptable to GOD save through JESUS CHRIST, it is very blessed to know how fully all his needs are met in CHRIST, and how truly he is accepted in Him, and enabled to give very real joy to GOD our FATHER, which issues in the bestowal of His richest blessings. Very imperfect—sometimes worse than useless, is the attempt of a little child to please and serve its parent; but where the parent sees an effort to do his will, and to give him pleasure, is not the service gladly accepted, and the parent's heart greatly rejoiced? Thus it is our privilege to be Nazarites, only and always Nazarites, and through CHRIST JESUS to give joy and satisfaction by our imperfect service to our heavenly FATHER. The following anonymous lines, taken from a leaflet, beautifully illustrate this thought:

THE PRESENTATION OF THE NAZARITE.

Let us now look into the law of the Nazarite when the days of his separation were fulfilled. The first thing that strikes our notice is, "He shall be brought," not, he shall come. Why is this? and why is it that the law is so explicit as to every detail of ritual and service, scarcely leaving any room for voluntary action?—we say *scarcely*, because in the twenty-first verse there is one little clause, "Beside that that his hand shall get," which does leave room for additional tokens of gratitude and love.

The answer seems to be, that the voluntary part of Nazarite service lay first and chiefly in the surrender to become a Nazarite. In that position he was not his own, as we have pointed out, and the MASTER whom he served naturally and consistently directed the service.

Again, does not, "He shall be brought" imply that, Nazarite as he was, he still needed priestly ministration to present himself, and his finished service, before the LORD? And our HIGH PRIEST, who is now able to keep us from falling to the end of our surrendered service, waits to present us with exceeding joy, "faultless before the presence of His glory"—"holy and unblameable and unreproveable in His sight."

THE LAW OF THE OFFERINGS.

When we come to the offerings enumerated in v. 14, we notice that they are mentioned in the almost invariable *order of enumeration*—first the burnt-offering, then the sin-offering, and lastly the peace offering; but when in v. 16 we come to the offering up of the sacrifices, we notice that *as always* the sin-offering is the *first to be offered.*

It is somewhat remarkable that the actual order of offering, and the order of enumeration should not correspond; and it is likewise noteworthy that the sacrifice which was always offered first, when offered at all, was *comparatively* insignificant in point of value, and much less frequently called for in the services

Separation and Service

of the Levitical ritual. For instance, in Numbers xxviii, xxix, the daily offering was a burnt-offering of a he-lamb morning and evening, with the corresponding accompaniments of fine flour mingled with oil, and a drink-offering of wine. On the Sabbath Day an additional burnt-offering of two lambs with their meat-offering and drink-offering was required. At the time of the new moon, the additional offering was of two bullocks, one ram, and seven lambs, with their meat and drink-offerings, for a burnt-offering, while one he-goat sufficed for a sin-offering. The same offerings were offered at the Feasts of Passover and Pentecost. On several other occasions the offerings were nearly of the same proportions; while during the Feast of Tabernacles the offerings commenced with thirteen bullocks, two rams, and fourteen lambs for a burnt-offering to one he-goat for a sin-offering.

The same disproportion of number and value may be noticed on many occasions between the sin-offering and the peace offering. A striking example of this was the sacrifice of peace-offerings made by Solomon on the dedication of the temple to the number of 22,000 oxen, and 120,000 sheep.

We cannot but see that teaching of the most important character is to be gathered from these facts; and is it not clear that while the need of forgiveness and cleansing is never to be lost sight of, it is *not* intended that a sense of the presence and defilement of sin should be the prominent feature of the service of GOD?

On the great Day of Atonement Israel's sin was confessed *and put away*; and thenceforward the daily and the Sabbath worship was that of whole burnt-offering. At the special festivals a he-goat was sacrificed for sin; but, as we have seen, the burnt-offerings, which speak of acceptance by, and devotion to, GOD were the principal features. It is the purpose of GOD that in the present dispensation His people should have and enjoy *full assurance* of salvation through the offering of JESUS CHRIST once for all; and more than this, should know that He who "died for their offences, and was raised again for their justification," henceforth "liveth unto GOD;" *in order* that His people may likewise "reckon themselves to be dead indeed unto sin, but alive unto GOD, in JESUS CHRIST our LORD."

In JESUS CHRIST there is no condemnation. In JESUS CHRIST, the law of the SPIRIT of life hath set me "free from the law of sin and of death." By the will of GOD "we are sanctified, through the offering of the body of JESUS CHRIST once for all;" and by "that one offering He hath perfected for ever them that are sanctified."

THE BURNT-OFFERING.

To return to the order of enumeration: the burnt-offering is always mentioned first, because it is the highest in character, and gave most pleasure to GOD. It was wholly the LORD's; no part of it was eaten by the priest who offered it, nor by the offerer who presented it, it was all and only for GOD's satisfaction. When Noah offered his burnt-offering, the LORD smelled a sweet savour, and blessed him and his posterity. When Abraham in purpose offered up his son Isaac, GOD said, "By myself have I sworn, saith the LORD, for because thou hast done this thing, ... that in blessing I will bless thee, and in multiplying I will multiply thy seed; ... and thy seed shall possess the gate of his enemies; and in thy seed shall all the nations of the earth be blessed."

The burnt-offering tells us of the perfect and accepted righteousness of CHRIST, in virtue of which the imperfect believer and his imperfect service are accepted by GOD. But it also reminds the believer of his privilege to *surrender himself* as a living sacrifice, holy and acceptable unto GOD, which is to be the reasonable (intelligent) service (that is, ritual or worship) of each day and hour.

THE SIN-OFFERING AND THE PEACE-OFFERING.

The sin-offering, as its name indicates, recognized the offerer as guilty and defiled, but obtaining forgiveness and cleansing through the death of the victim in his stead. We see Christ as our sin-offering in Isa. liii. 4-10. But guilt removed still leaves the believer needing the imputed righteousness of Christ, and acceptance before God, which are the aspects of Christ's death foreshadowed, as we have seen by the burnt-offering.

Lastly, the peace-offering—part of which was consumed on the altar, while part was the portion of the priest, and the remainder furnished a feast to the offerer and his friends—shows us God and man feasting together on the perfect work of Christ. He that sanctifieth and those who are sanctified, find their full satisfaction in Him, and in Him alone. He has made peace by the blood of His cross. He has given us His own peace. We are called to let His peace *rule* in our hearts. And if we will but bring our burdens and cares to Him, we are promised that the peace of God shall guard and garrison our hearts and thoughts in Christ Jesus!

PART II
The Blessing of GOD

NUMB. VI. 22-27.

WE HAVE ALREADY SEEN the grace of GOD making provision that His people, who had lost the privilege of priestly service, might draw near to Him by Nazarite separation and consecration. And not as the offence was the free gift: those who had forfeited the privilege of priestly service were the males only, but women and even children might be Nazarites; whosoever desired was free to come, and thus draw near to GOD.

We now come to the concluding verses of Numb. vi, and see in them one of the fullest forms of benediction to be found in the whole Word of GOD. The thought naturally arises,

WHY IS IT FOUND HERE?

And the reply is twofold. There is the Divine side. Flowing from GOD'S heart of love first came the *privilege* of Nazarite consecration; and then, by the *act* of consecration, His loving heart is so gladdened that it further overflows in these rich benedictions.

Looking, on the other hand, at the human side, we may learn that the soul which is fully consecrated *always* receives the blessing of GOD. Where that blessing is not enjoyed, there is always something unreal or defective in the consecration. It may be that we have separated ourselves to carry out *our own will, or thought, or plan of service,* instead of surrendering ourselves and *our* will, to learn and to do *His* will. But it is real consecration *to GOD* that puts us into the position in which He can pour out His richest blessings upon us.

The prodigal was a son of the father all the time; but when he preferred *his* will

Separation and Service

to the will of his father, *his* way to the way of his father, *his* management of his share in the property to his father's management, it issued but in ruin and misery—in hunger and nakedness and shame.

The fact that he was a son was of no avail to him in the "far country," in the place of self-will and self-management. But as soon as he arose, and with true repentance and submission came back to the father's house, willing to serve, and to do his father's will, he found himself restored to his father's heart, and to all the privileges of sonship: the fatted calf was killed, the best robe was put upon him, once more he had shoes on his feet and a ring on his hand, and joy and gladness filled the home.

How many Christians there are who, in their self-will and attempted self-management, find themselves day by day full of sorrow, or full of care. Trying to keep themselves they are not kept; trying to be happy they are often unhappy; trying to succeed they fail; and they can but confess that their life is very different from that ideal life described in Ps. lxxxix. 15-18:

Instead of this many practically know very little of peace "which passeth all understanding," of joy that is literally "unspeakable"; adjectives far more moderate would be found strong enough to express all *they* know of oft-troubled peace and intermittent satisfaction and happiness.

Many there are who fail to see that there can be but one lord, and that those who do not make GOD *Lord of all* do not make Him *Lord at all*. The slightest reservation in our consecration shows that we hold ourselves *as our own*, and consequently at liberty to give Him as much or as little as we think fit.

If we recognize Him as LORD and MASTER, we have nothing to withhold, and nothing of our own, for we, and all we have, are already His. But then, in return, all He has, and all He is, become ours. Oh! blessed PORTION! Who would not wish henceforth to have no private property in himself—in his members—in his possessions—in his family—in his affections; but, in fullest consecration, to acknowledge and recognize GOD'S right and to be no longer a robber of GOD?

"And the LORD spake unto Moses, saying, Speak unto Aaron and unto his sons, saying, On this wise ye shall bless the children of Israel ... And they shall put My Name upon the children of Israel; and I will bless them."

Here we have the blessing that GOD *delights* to give to those who have dedicated themselves and their all to Him. Before considering it in detail, let us notice, first, how spontaneous and unsought is this blessing from GOD—the LORD *commanded* Aaron and his sons to bless Israel, to put His Name upon them; and declared His own unalterable purpose, "I *will* bless them." And then, let us ask ourselves the question, what is

THE REAL MEANING OF BLESSING?

We frequently use the word so vaguely as to lose much of its preciousness, and to overlook the primary meaning in some of its secondary significations. For instance, we use it frequently as a synonym of praise, and in speaking of blessing GOD, we think of praising Him. But blessing does not merely mean praise, for GOD blesses us.

Again, sometimes we use it for some gracious gift, as when we speak of the blessing of peace or of plenty.

But blessing does not only signify gift, for when we bless GOD we do not give to Him peace or plenty. Blessing is *the moving of the heart towards an object of affection and complacency*. The out-going of the heart is naturally *accompanied* by gift or ascription, as the case may be.

When our hearts bless the LORD, we sing a song of praise to Him for the great love wherewith He hath loved us; but the blessing is not the song—it is the feeling that prompts it. When the LORD blesses His people with peace and plenty, it is His open Heart that moves His loving Hand.

Again, blessing is always accompanied with joy; it *is* a joy, and it *gives* joy, both to the giver and the receiver. A little child playing with his toys may be both happy and satisfied. But it hears the mother's

Separation and Service

footsteps, it sees the mother open the door, and instantly the toys are dropped and forgotten; the little arms are stretched out, and the little feet are running to meet the welcome mother.

Nor is this all; the great, motherly arms are as quickly stretched forth towards the child, and with longer steps the mother hastens to meet the little one, and clasps it to her bosom, the loving little arms entwining themselves around her neck.

But whose heart is the more glad? The little one's heart is *full*; and the mother's heart is also *full*; but her capacity is greater, and so her joy is deeper. And is not this true of our HEAVENLY FATHER? When His heart blesses ours, and ours blesses HIM, *we* are full of joy; but His heart is infinitely greater than ours, and His joy in His people as far exceeds all their joy in Him, as the infinite exceeds the finite.

Let us always remember in connection with blessing that the deep heart-feeling is the primary thought. "Bless the LORD, O my *soul*; and all that is *within me*, bless His holy Name." The praise of the lip may be insincere; the blessing of the heart cannot be.

THE THREE-FOLD BENEDICTION: verses 24-26.

"The LORD bless thee, and keep thee:
"The LORD make His face shine upon thee, and be gracious unto thee:
"The LORD lift up His countenance upon thee, and give thee peace."

We have dwelt upon the meaning of blessing—the moving of the heart towards an object of affection and complacency, and noticed that this is naturally accompanied by gift or ascription, as the case may be. When love overflows, loving words, loving embraces, or loving gifts instinctively follow.

In the light of the fuller revelation of the New Testament we can scarcely fail to see in this three-fold benediction the overflow in blessing of the FATHER, of the SON, and of the SPIRIT; and we may read it as follows:—

"JEHOVAH, THE FATHER, BLESS THEE, AND KEEP THEE:

"JEHOVAH, THE SON, THE BRIDEGROOM, MAKE HIS FACE SHINE UPON THEE, AND BE GRACIOUS UNTO THEE:

"JEHOVAH, THE SPIRIT, LIFT UP HIS COUNTENANCE UPON THEE, AND GIVE THEE PEACE."

So read, we see in these words fuller beauty and appropriateness. Let us now notice the first clause in particular.

THE BLESSING OF THE FATHER.

Considered as a father's blessing could anything be more appropriate than "The LORD bless thee, and keep thee"? Is not this just what every loving father seeks to do—to bless and keep his children? He does not find it an unwelcome task, but his greatest delight. Offer to relieve him of the responsibility and to adopt his child, and see what his reply will be! Nor may we confine ourselves to paternal love in thinking of this subject; but rather take it as parental love, embracing also the love of the mother, for "Thus saith the LORD, ... As one whom his mother comforteth, so will I comfort you." We all know how the mother-love delights to lavish itself on the objects of its care.

With a patience that never tires, and an endurance almost inexhaustible, and a care all but unlimited, how often has the mother sacrificed her very life for the welfare of her babe. But strong as is a mother's love, it *may* fail; GOD'S love *never*. "Can a woman forget her suckling child that she should not have compassion on the son of her womb? yea, they may forget, yet will I not forget thee."

It was one of the objects of our SAVIOUR'S mission to reveal to us that, in CHRIST JESUS, GOD is also our FATHER. How He delighted in bringing out this precious truth the Sermon on the Mount bears witness: "Glorify your Father." "Love ... bless ... do good, that ye may be the children of your FATHER." Be "perfect, even as your FATHER." "Thy FATHER ... seeth." "Your FATHER knoweth," etc., etc. And well may our hearts rest in the thought which so satisfied His heart, that

Separation and Service

GOD is indeed our FATHER.

And what a glorious FATHER He is! the source of all true fatherhood and motherhood. We have often walked in the fields in the early morning, and have noticed how the rising sun has turned each dewdrop into a glittering gem; one ray of its own bright light makes a little sun of each of the million drops that hang from the pendent leaflets and sparkle everywhere.

But it is helpful to remember that the glorious orb itself contains infinitely more light than all the dewdrops ever did or ever will reflect. And so of our heavenly FATHER: Himself the great Source of all that is noble and true, of all that ever has been loving and trustworthy—each beautiful trait of each beautiful character is but the dim reflection of some ray of His own great perfection. And the sum-total of all human goodness, and tenderness, and love is but as the dewdrops to the sun. How blessed then to confide in the infinite and changeless love of such a FATHER—our FATHER in heaven!

How safe too! "There is none like unto the GOD of Jeshurun, who rideth upon the heaven in thy help, and in His excellency on the sky. The eternal GOD is thy refuge, and underneath are the everlasting arms." Ofttimes where the love of earthly parents has not failed, yet have they been powerless to bless and to keep. The cruel tyrant has tortured the parent in torturing the child; while there has been no power to deliver. And in the presence of human want or suffering how impotent has the strongest human love oft proved to be! Not so the love of our heavenly FATHER: His resources and His power are as inexhaustible as His love; and they are blest and kept indeed whom He deigns to bless and keep.

May we not add "they only"? The foolish prodigal imagines that he can secure greater happiness for himself when no longer curbed by his father's presence and will; such always come to want, and, alas! do not always return quickly to the home where reconciliation and blessing alone are to be found. He is poorly kept who tries to keep himself;

Separation and Service

and though the pleasures of sin may for a season gratify, they can never satisfy!B

"JEHOVAH, the FATHER, bless *thee*, and keep *thee*." It is an individual blessing: and it includes every form of blessing, temporal as well as spiritual —"My GOD shall supply all your need"; and this "according to His riches in glory in CHRIST JESUS," not according to our consciousness of need. He is *able* to bless, able to make all grace abound—to so wonderfully abound towards us, that we always having all sufficiency in all things, may abound to every good work: He is able to keep—to keep us from falling, to keep us from all evil. And not only is He able, but He has already "blessed us with all spiritual blessings in heavenly things in CHRIST," and He wants us, His children, to know and to enjoy the love that is the source of all blessing: the love that can never by finite words express its fulness: the love that eternal ages will never exhaust!

* When we speak of GOD as a FATHER we must not forget that He is only such in its full meaning to those who have become His children by faith in CHRIST JESUS; and that the sad and solemn words of the loving Saviour to the unconverted were, "Ye are of *your* father, the devil." The prodigal was a backslider: when furthest from home he could yet think and speak of the privileges of his father's house.

THE SECOND PERSON OF THE TRINITY.

The second clause of the blessing is the blessing of the SON, which is not less full and appropriate. Through eternal ages the SON of GOD, He became, in the fulness of time, the SON of Man. The Brightness of His FATHER'S glory, the SUN of Righteousness, He came to manifest, as well as to speak of, the FATHER'S love. He became the LIGHT of the world, as well as the LAMB of GOD; but in each aspect doing the will, as well as the work of GOD, He thus revealed the wondrous love and grace of the FATHER, and His own perfect Sonship. The FATHER'S will included CHRIST'S glad reception of all who come to

Separation and Service

Him, His meeting all their need—saving, sanctifying, satisfying, keeping, raising up at the last day—His giving Himself for, and giving Himself to, all those given to Him of the FATHER.

He is indeed a wonderful Saviour! What light the incarnate WORD of GOD (Who is Light) has thrown on the written Word of GOD! The law in its legal requirements He has fulfilled, bringing in everlasting righteousness, which is imputed to all those who are indeed in Him. He has also fulfilled the Law in its manifold typical aspects—Himself the Temple, the Priest, and the Sacrifice; Himself the Altar, the Offerer, and the Victim; Himself the Lamp, and the Priestly Trimmer of the lamps (as He is also the whole Vine, and yet the Life of each individual branch of the Vine).

Time would fail us to enumerate the various objects and acts of typical service which were all fulfilled in Him. He too is the BRIDEGROOM, from whose wounded side the Bride is being formed; and He is waiting for His Bride, who will soon be caught up to meet Him in the air. The true

SOLOMON is He whose glory we shall share, and not only so, but whose presence will be the ever-satisfying portion of His chosen Bride.

May the HOLY SPIRIT give us more and more to realize the practical bearing of all that is thus revealed of the glory of the Person, and the fulness of the work of our SAVIOUR and KING!

THE BLESSING OF THE SON AND BRIDEGROOM.

JEHOVAH, THE SON, MAKE HIS FACE SHINE UPON THEE, AND BE GRACIOUS UNTO THEE.

The first clause of the three-fold blessing told of the going out of the heart of the invisible FATHER; now, when we come to the blessing of the SON, we read, "The LORD *make his face shine* upon thee," or, in other words, make visibly *manifest* His favour towards thee.

The SON of GOD is the KINSMAN who has the right to redeem, the FRIEND who sticketh closer than a brother, the ONE who has come, not only to be the LIGHT of the world, but in an especial sense to be the LIGHT of His own redeemed ones.

There was no need in Israel of a kinsman-redeemer in times of prosperity; but when bereavement and poverty afforded opportunity to the creditors to seize the possession, then a kind and wealthy kinsman-redeemer was a blessing indeed. We are reminded of the beautiful history of Ruth: how sweetly the gracious words of Boaz fell on the ear of the young stranger, and what blessing that kinsman brought into her heart and life! The FRIEND that sticketh closer than a brother is precious at all times, but never so valued as in times of adversity; and the very expression, "THE LIGHT of the world," tells us of the darkness that sin has brought in—a darkness, alas! not only around, but also within.

The shining of the face of JEHOVAH, the SON, dispels the darkness and the gloom, manifests the presence of the FRIEND in need, and shows us the REDEEMER, who not only delivers, but becomes the BRIDEGROOM of the soul.

"Make His *face* shine upon thee." The face is perhaps the most wonderful part of the wonderful human body. Of all the faces that GOD has made no two are exactly alike, even when quiescent; and though we do occasionally meet with those that bear a very close resemblance, intimate friends, who know the play of the countenance, never mistake. And why is this? Because GOD has so ordered it, that the face shall *reveal* the character and feelings of the individual.

And it is the purpose of GOD that the heart of CHRIST shall be revealed to His people. That heart might have been full of love, and we might never have known it; but it is the will of GOD that "the light of the knowledge of the glory of GOD" should be *revealed* to us "in the face of JESUS CHRIST."

How well we know in actual life what the light of the countenance means! How the mother's smile brings light and gladness into the heart of the child! How the welcoming look of a friend is at once understood! In Daniel ix. 16, 17, the prophet prays, "O Lord ... I beseech Thee, let Thine anger and Thy fury be turned away from Thy city, Jerusalem; ... and

Separation and Service

cause Thy face to shine upon Thy sanctuary that is desolate." Where there is the shining of the face we know there is more than forgiveness; there is favour and complacence. In the thrice-offered prayer of Psalm lxxx, "Cause Thy face to shine, and we shall be saved," the salvation of Israel is counted upon as the result; and in Psalm lxvii, we find that the shining of GOD'S face upon His people is further to issue in His way being "known upon earth, His saving health among all nations."

It is, however, when we consider Him in the relationship of BRIDEGROOM and KING that the tenderness and preciousness of this blessing are most fully seen. A truly royal BRIDEGROOM: "in His favour is life," and to Him we can approach at all times, without any fear that He will hide His countenance, or that He will not hold out to us the golden sceptre. Queen Esther might tremble for the result of her boldness, but our KING ever welcomes the approach of His Bride.

When her heart cries out, "Let him kiss me with the kisses of His mouth," He is ever ready to bring her into His chambers; indeed it is often the BRIDEGROOM who has to allure the Bride,[C] rather than the Bride who has to seek the favour of the BRIDEGROOM. It is only when she has treated him with neglect or disobedience that she finds herself in darkness. And what is not His favour to a loyal and true-hearted Bride! To a subject, the favour of the KING is "as dew upon the grass," but to a bride is it not everything? "JEHOVAH, the BRIDEGROOM, make His face shine upon thee, and be gracious unto thee!"

What a wonderful view of the light of His countenance the favoured disciples must have had, who were witnesses of His transfiguration: we are told that His face did shine as the sun. To the proto-martyr Stephen the heavens were opened, and the face of the LORD shone upon him: and when he saw Him he became so like Him, that his dying utterances corresponded with those of his LORD on the Cross. When Saul, likewise, saw the glory of his risen SAVIOUR, on the way to Damascus, the vision at midday was of a light above the brightness of the sun shining round about him; and the effect of that heavenly vision changed the whole current of his life, making him a follower of the CHRIST, who pleased not Himself, and making the spirit manifested in his first cry, "LORD, what wilt *Thou* have me to do?" the spirit of his life ever after. And so when the LORD makes the light of His countenance to shine upon any of His people, in the measure in which with unveiled face they discern the beauty of the LORD, there is a moral and progressive change into His likeness, the work of the LORD, the SPIRIT.

"Rise up, my love, my fair one, and come away."—Cant. ii. 10;

"Come with Me from Lebanon, My spouse."—Cant. iv. 8.

THE LORD, THE SPIRIT.

We have considered the bountiful overflow of the FATHER's love; and our hearts have burned within us as we dwelt upon and felt the glow of the love of the SON. Now, as we think of the blessing of the LORD, the SPIRIT, may He reveal Himself to us through these holy Words, which were written by His inspiration and which can never be fully understood and enjoyed save by His own illumination. The Bible is a supernatural book, a divine revelation: the HOLY SPIRIT is the supernatural, the divine GUIDE to its meaning. From the "wise and prudent" its teachings are hidden;—hence the questionings of some of the learned only confirm its truth; but to "babes"—to all those, whether learned or unlearned, in whom the HOLY GHOST has wrought the child-like spirit, it is an opened book: they love it, and feast upon it, and grow thereby.

It is very important to have clear thoughts about the third person of the Trinity. Many Christians fail in this respect, and lose much in consequence. He has as distinct personality as has the SON of GOD; and we must not think or speak of Him vaguely, as though He were an influence merely and not a person. Our SAVIOUR teaches us that *we* should *know* Him, "for He abideth with you, and shall be in you." But are there not many of the LORD'S people to whom He is not yet "a living, bright Reality"?

So important are the presence and the work of the HOLY GHOST, that our LORD assured His disciples that it was expedient for them that *He* should go away, in order that the COMFORTER should come. And we see the mighty change that was wrought in the disciples when the outpouring of the SPIRIT actually took place at Pentecost. The timid became courageous; the scattered and persecuted disciples went everywhere preaching the Word; the HOLY SPIRIT wrought conviction of sin, and revealed the risen SAVIOUR as the object of faith; and many were added to the LORD. The same SPIRIT is still present with us; may we too be filled, and largely used as channels of blessing.

THE BLESSING OF THE HOLY SPIRIT.

"JEHOVAH, THE SPIRIT, LIFT UP HIS COUNTENANCE UPON THEE, AND GIVE THEE PEACE."

The blessing of the SPIRIT is essential to the completeness of the benediction. We are struck, however, with the similarity of this blessing to that which precedes it; nor is the similarity surprising. For, as the SON came to reveal the FATHER, so the SPIRIT has come to reveal the SON. CHRIST was a true COMFORTER; but His personal work on earth being finished, He ascended on high to minister for His people as their HIGH PRIEST in the presence of GOD. The HOLY SPIRIT is the other COMFORTER, sent by the FATHER in CHRIST'S name, that He might abide with the Church for ever. CHRIST is the indwelling SAVIOUR: the HOLY SPIRIT the indwelling COMFORTER. On whomsoever CHRIST makes His face to shine, the HOLY SPIRIT will surely lift up

HIS COUNTENANCE.

"Lift up His *countenance* upon thee."

We have already dwelt on the significance of the face or countenance (the same original word) as revealing the emotions of the heart. We see from these words that it is the purpose of GOD that the presence and the love of the SPIRIT should be made known to those in whom He dwells. When He lifts up His countenance upon us, we walk in conscious security and freedom; but if the SPIRIT be grieved, the light of His countenance is hidden from us, and we walk in darkness.

And, oh, how dangerous is this walking in darkness, how surely we shall wander from the way, and fall into some of the snares of the devil! There is only one safe course, to confess the sin that has grieved Him, and take no rest till communion is restored: this may always be done most easily by *immediate* confession and turning to Him, who is our Advocate with the FATHER, and whose shed blood cleanses from all sin. When sin is put away the SPIRIT again lifts up His countenance upon us, and peace fills the heart.

THE PEACE OF THE SPIRIT.

The LORD JESUS, when on earth, said,

"Peace I leave with you, My peace I give unto you: not as the world giveth, give I unto you. Let not your heart be troubled, neither let it be afraid."

But here it is the SPIRIT who is spoken of as bestowing peace: why is this? Because the SPIRIT of GOD makes real things real to *us*, and enables us practically to enjoy the blessings procured for us by the death and resurrection and priestly ministry of the LORD JESUS. Many a believer to whom CHRIST has left peace, knows little of it; but those who are filled with the SPIRIT are filled with peace. They have peace with GOD; they have also heart-peace in the midst of conflict and turmoil; and the peace of GOD, which passeth all understanding, guards their hearts and thoughts. The fruit of the SPIRIT is love, joy, peace.

Are *we* practically enjoying this blessing, and experiencing this peace which passes all understanding? Are we *finding* that when He makes quietness, none can make trouble? And if not, what is the hindrance? Is there any known sin unconfessed, or not put away? Has wrong been done, and restitution to the extent of our ability not been made?

Is there any matter in which GOD has a controversy with us? Or are we indulging ourselves in anything about which we have doubt? Are we withholding anything from GOD which is His due—ourselves, our property, our children; or, it may be, our testimony? Or, if none of these things are hindering us, are we failing to *accept*, by faith, the filling of the SPIRIT; perhaps only asking, but not receiving also? Is it that we are neglecting the prayerful study of GOD'S Word, and thus grieving the SPIRIT by whom it was inspired?

Paul asked GOD to give the Ephesian Christians the SPIRIT of wisdom and revelation in the knowledge of CHRIST, that they might know the hope of His calling and the exceeding greatness of His power toward them *that believe*. We do well to note the words "that believe," for unbelief lies at the root of every form of hindrance.

As the SPIRIT reveals CHRIST, so does CHRIST bestow the SPIRIT; and by faith in

CHRIST and in His Word we appropriate the gift. We shall never forget the blessing we received through the words, in John iv. 14, "Whosoever drinketh of the water that I shall give him

SHALL NEVER THIRST,"

nearly thirty years ago. As we realized that CHRIST literally meant what He said—that "shall" meant shall, and "never" meant never, and "thirst" meant thirst—our heart overflowed with joy as we accepted the gift. Oh, the thirst with which we had sat down, but oh, the joy with which we sprang from our seat, praising the LORD that the thirsting days were all past, and past for ever! For, as our LORD continues, "the water that I shall give him shall be *in him* a well of water, springing up—overflowing—unto everlasting life."

Perhaps, however, we should draw attention to the words of CHRIST, "whosoever drinketh"; not drank—once for all—but "drinketh," that is habitually: as in chap. vii. 38, 39, where, after promising that out of him "shall flow rivers of living water," it is significally added, "this spake He of the SPIRIT, which they that believe"—*i.e.*, keep believing—should receive.

Is it not sad that so free a gift should be so little esteemed, so often neither enjoyed nor sought after? It is intended for *each one* of us—"lift up His countenance upon *thee*, and give *thee* peace." Would that each reader would accept the gift *now*, and evermore enjoy it, to the glory of GOD.

SEALING WITH THE NAME OF GOD: verse 27.

"And they shall put My Name upon the children of Israel; and I will bless them."

With these words this wonderful chapter closes, and the great object of GOD in bestowing His blessing upon His people is revealed: "They shall put *My Name* upon the children of Israel," or, in other words, shall cause them not only to become the people of GOD, but also to become manifestly such.

In olden time names were not meaningless, but were descriptive of character or relationship. The various names of GOD are all full of significance, and each is always used designedly in the Bible: failing to recognize this, learned, but spiritually-ignorant men have imagined the Old Testament writings to have been mere compilations from the works of different authors, and have failed to see the beautiful appropriateness of the various names of GOD as they are used in different connections.

In the preceding benediction the thrice repeated Name of JEHOVAH has revealed to us the triune GOD in His gracious relations with His redeemed people, and has also reminded us that in these relationships He is the unchanging One, the same yesterday, to-day, and for ever; for all this is contained in the Name JEHOVAH. And thus the expression, "They shall put *My Name* upon the children of Israel," implies the purpose of GOD that in His people should be manifested, not only the *beauties* of His Divine character, but also

Separation and Service

the *unchanging relationship* in which they stand to Him. Israel of old was, and still is, GOD'S witness in the world.

In all their unfaithfulness, their very existence as a separate people is a standing miracle, witnessing to the truth of prophecy. But had they been faithful they would have been much more than this; for the beauty of the LORD their GOD would have been upon them; and receiving His blessing themselves, they would have become a blessing to the world.

We who are now the children of GOD—Christians upon whom the Name of CHRIST has been called—are intended to be witnesses for our MASTER, and to show forth the beauties of Him who has "called us by His own glory and virtue." (2 Peter i. 3.—R.V.)

There is an interesting parallelism between the passage we are considering and the commission given by our LORD to His people to disciple all nations, baptizing them into the *Name* of the FATHER, the SON, and the HOLY GHOST. True Christians are *kept* by the power of GOD ("the LORD bless thee and *keep thee*"), in the grace which is in CHRIST JESUS ("the LORD make His face shine upon thee, and be *gracious unto thee*"), and receive the illumination of the HOLY GHOST ("the LORD *lift up His countenance upon thee*"), in order that *they* may shine as lights in the world, and become living epistles, known and read of all men.

It is deeply interesting also to connect the sealing of this passage with that of Rev. vii and xiv. In the former passage (Rev. vii. 1-3) we see the powers to whom the plagues are committed restrained until the sealing of the servants of GOD is completed.

The hundred and forty and four thousand are all sealed—a mystical and symbolical number of the mystical and symbolical Israel, not of Israel according to the flesh. For in this book of Revelation the LAMB does not mean an animal, but the LAMB of GOD. The beast does not mean a literal wild beast, but the spiritual wild beast who destroys the children of GOD. So the twelve thousand of the tribe of Judah refers to the praising ones of

CHRIST'S fold; the sealed of Asher to the happy ones, who bless the LORD at all times; those of Naphtali, to those satisfied with favour, full with the blessing of the LORD; those of Reuben, to the once unstable as water, but now fully saved ones; &c., &c.

In Rev. xiii we find the great tribulation in progress, and those still left on the earth persecuted sorely, many of them to the death, by the beast. But the hundred forty and four thousand of Rev. xiv are not among them; they were caught up before the tribulation commenced, having been accounted worthy (Luke xxi. 34-36), to escape the things coming on the earth, and to stand before the SON of MAN.

Such are not only virgins, undefiled by spiritual adultery with the world, but also wise ones, filled with the SPIRIT: they are not only waiting for the coming of the Bridegroom, but ready for that coming; whereas the unwise have to go and buy oil, and so miss their opportunity.

In Rev. xiv we see that GOD'S Name is written on the foreheads of these wise virgins, and that in their mouths is a song which no one else can sing. They are a first-fruits Bride united to the first-fruit's Bridegroom, and were redeemed (not from among the Jews only, but from among men), unto GOD and the LAMB. Other believers, then in the tribulation, shall join them later and form the harvest unto GOD (Rev. vii. 14-17), and will come with the Bridegroom and Bride when our LORD is revealed from heaven in flaming fire to take vengeance on the ungodly (2 Thess. i, 6-10).

The harvest is not only separated from the first-fruits in Rev. vii and xiv, but also in Rev. xx. We may read verses 4-6 more clearly if we render the second clause of verse 4, "I saw also the souls of them, &c.," instead of "and I saw, &c." and the last clause, "They also lived and reigned with CHRIST a thousand years." We thus see the enthroned Bridegroom and Bride and the harvest, the Body of CHRIST, forming the first resurrection, and together reigning in glory.

"And I will bless them." A word of encouragement to Aaron and his sons in pronouncing the blessing, as well as to

the people who received it. The blessing was preceded by GOD'S command ("Speak unto Aaron ... On this wise ye shall bless"), and followed by the promise quoted above; even as our SAVIOUR in giving His last commission to disciple all nations, preceded it by, "All power is given unto Me...: Go ye therefore;" and followed it by the assurance and promise, "Lo, I am with you alway."

In the word of a King there is power; and when His servants carry out His commands, our KING is present to authenticate them, and to ensure the result.

PART III
Princely Service

NUMB. VII

WE LEARNED FROM Numbers vi, GOD'S requirements of those who desire to take the privileged position of separation to Himself. We found also in the conclusion of the same chapter the overflow of GOD'S love in the rich and comprehensive blessing which so appropriately follows, and forms the connecting link between Nazarite separation and the princely service set forth in Chap. vii,—one of the longest in the Bible, and one full of repetition. We now propose to consider more fully why this service of giving finds such lengthy record.

J Hudson Taylor

SERVICE THE CONSTRAINT OF LOVE.

Is it not that just as separation to GOD issues in blessing, so does blessing from GOD constrain to service, and especially to the highest form of service, that which is most GOD-like, that of *Giving*? GOD so loved the world that He *gave*; CHRIST so loved the Church that He *gave*; the HOLY SPIRIT so loves the Church that He *gives*; and redeemed ones, created anew in CHRIST JESUS unto good works, when led by the SPIRIT, first *give* themselves unto GOD, and then delight in such other free-will offerings as the LORD may enable them to present. This we believe is the reason why the chapter is found here, and is the true connection between its subject-matter and that of the preceding one.

But why is it so long, so repetitious, and so tedious? The Bible is a wonderful book; it not only gives the history of the past, and guidance for the present, but in prophecy we have the history of ages yet to come—the course of events until the grand climax when GOD shall be all in all.

Why, in a book so marvellous in its comprehensiveness, is so much space given to this record?

GOD'S DELIGHT IN LOVE-GIFTS.

Is it not in order to reveal the heart of GOD? to show His delight in the loving offerings of His servants? The record is *not* tedious to Him; and it becomes marvellously interesting to us, when we get the key, and are brought into sympathy with the heart of Him who finds infinite satisfaction in each gift, of each one of His children, which is the outcome of gratitude and love.

In the days of our LORD'S life on earth, when the shadow of the cross was already upon Him, one only amongst all His followers—a woman, Mary—had understood and really taken in His repeated declaration of the sufferings that awaited Him; and when she came to anoint Him beforehand for the burial, and broke the precious alabaster box *she had reserved for this very purpose*, the thief who kept the bag had only angry words of criticism and reproach. How sweet to her wounded spirit was her MASTER'S commendation, "She hath done what she could!" And He added, "Wheresoever this Gospel shall be preached throughout the whole world, this also that she hath done shall be spoken of for a memorial of her."

On an earlier occasion, likewise, as He sat over against the treasury, many that were rich cast in large sums of silver and of gold, but He turned from them and their gifts to draw attention to a certain poor widow who brought two mites and cast them in. She had gladdened the heart of Him who was the Creator of all wealth, and the real Owner of it all. She, said He, had given more than they all: for she *of her want* had given *all* that she had! And of her, as of Mary, it is true that in whatsoever language the Word of GOD is translated, in whatsoever clime it is read, the MASTER'S commendation is made known.

There is a day coming, in which before assembled worlds He will make manifest the loving gifts and the secret service of His redeemed ones. Then we shall not

Separation and Service

weary as they are recounted and rewarded; and as we see His joy in them all, we shall better understand the length of Numbers vii.

FREE-WILL OFFERINGS: verses 1, 2.

"And it came to pass on the day that Moses had fully set up the tabernacle, and had anointed it, and sanctified it ... and all the vessels thereof, ... that the princes of Israel, heads of the house of their fathers, ... offered."

When the LORD gave the plan of the tabernacle and of the vessels, He likewise gave to the people willing hearts to offer, and skill to execute. There was no need to press them; the workers and contributors were those whose heart stirred them up, and whose spirit was made willing. The people brought more than enough for the service of the work, and Moses had to make proclamation throughout the camp to restrain them from bringing more.

Is there not a lesson to be learnt here? Let the work only be one of GOD'S planning, and executed according to His mind, and the hearts that are in sympathy with Him will gladly respond with suitable and abundant offerings. For is not the willingness to give as much a part of His working as the skill to use that which is given? Then, in the givers and in their gifts, in the workers and in their work, the Divine heart finds infinite complacency. "For of Him," as the great Designer, "and through Him," as the effectual Power for the carrying out of His purposes, "and to Him," as the real Object of all service, "are all things: to whom be the glory for ever. Amen."

But divine service requires not only initiating, but also maintaining worthily of GOD. It was not sufficient that the tabernacle and the vessels of ministry were according to the divine pattern, both as to material and workmanship, and that they were made by divinely qualified workmen; but when all was completed and fully set up, both the tabernacle and the vessels needed anointing and sanctifying; and *when that was done* the offerings needed to carry on the service could not but be freely poured in. In like manner in all life and work, individual or organised, only let GOD have His right place, and let there be *the anointing* of the HOLY GHOST, received by faith, as well as consecration to Him, and everything will follow, as needful, for the carrying out of GOD'S plan in the life or work.

GLADSOME ACCEPTANCE: verses 3-5.

"And they brought their offering before the LORD, six covered wagons, and twelve oxen; ... and the LORD spake unto Moses, saying, Take it of them, that they may be to do the service of the tabernacle of the congregation; and thou shall give them unto the Levites, to every man according to his service."

It is interesting to note that the first offerings recorded were for the purpose of assisting in the moving of the tabernacle; it was not GOD'S purpose that it should be stationary. Nor is GOD'S work ever intended to be stationary, but always advancing.

The offerings themselves were remarkable: rude bullock-wagons, probably rough both in material and workmanship, much like those we now are familiar with in the unchanging East; they must have presented a striking contrast to the beauty of the skilfully prepared vessels of ministry. We may well imagine the thought to have passed through the mind of Moses, Can such rude offerings be acceptable to the glorious GOD? But GOD Himself dispels all doubt, by saying, "Take it of them."

GOD is not hard to please, nor is true human love, for it is a dim reflection of His own. We do not estimate our love-gifts by their intrinsic value, but rather by the love they express. Well do we remember a little incident which occurred some twenty-four years ago, and which illustrates this truth.

My little daughter, then about five years old, came to me on the morning of my birthday with a curious little birthday gift in her hand,—"Papa, I haven't bought you a birthday present," said she; "I thought

Separation and Service

you would rather have something I made myself." How my heart went out to the little darling, and how glad I was that she should think that something she could make would be more precious to me than any purchased gift! But what the curious little gift could be intended for I was quite at a loss to divine, and I engaged her in conversation, hoping she might let some clue slip that would help me to find out for what she meant it, for I feared she would be disappointed if I did not recognize it. The little pet had found a small piece of wood, and had bored a hole in it with her scissors, in which she had inserted a peg, and on the top had hung half a cockle-shell—certainly an uncommon birthday present!

At last, unable to guess what it was supposed to be, I took my dear child on my knee, and, kissing her, said, "Papa is so pleased to have a birthday present of your own making; what is it my darling has made for me?" "Why, don't you know, papa? I thought you would like best a ship to take you to China!"

The dear child was right; probably no

gift I ever received gave more pleasure, or was as carefully treasured, and as often thought of.

When that dear child had become old enough to engage in missionary work in China herself, and was able to introduce me to the first two Chinese women whom she had brought to CHRIST, I remembered the little ship; and when the women were gone reminded her about it, and told her that the joy of finding her now used of GOD in the blessed work itself was a greater joy than her gift had been. She was surprised that I should remember it; but it had never passed from my memory, and the recollection of it is a pleasure still. It is not hard to please those who love us.[D]

GOD *wants our love*; "My son, give Me thine heart." He wants our *sympathy*; He wants the gifts and offerings that are prompted by *love*. Shall He look to us in vain? Our David still thirsts, not for the waters of the well of Bethlehem, but for the souls for which He died. Shall He not have them? He specially needs willing, skilful young men, ready to break through

Separation and Service

the enemy's camp to deliver the captives of the mighty one. Who that can will go? Who that cannot go at present will help others to go?

* While preparing these sheets for the press we learn from a telegram that He whom my dear daughter had served in China since 1885, has called her (and her baby of sixteen months) from her husband, the Rev. J. J. Coulthard, and three surviving children, to the eternal home above.

ACCORDING TO HIS SERVICE:
verses 5-9.

"Thou shall give them unto the Levites, to every man according to his service. And Moses took the wagons and the oxen, and gave them unto the Levites. Two wagons and four oxen he gave unto the sons of Gershon, according to their service, and four wagons and eight oxen he gave unto the sons of Merari, according unto their service, under the hand of Ithamar the son of Aaron the priest. But unto the sons of

Kohath he gave none; because the service of the sanctuary belonging unto them was that they should bear upon their shoulders."

The princes brought their offering to the LORD, and the LORD accepted it. Having accepted it Himself it was His to give to whom He would; and He chose to give it to the Levites, for they in a special manner were His, and devoted to His service.

The tribe of Levi was in one sense the poorest in Israel. In dividing the land among the tribes, no territory was allotted to them. They will have territory by-and-by, when the LORD comes (*see* Ezek. xlviii. 12-14), but never have they had any yet. Cities to dwell in, and suburbs, were given them here and there, in all the tribes of Israel, but of earthly portion that was all.

And yet they were the richest tribe in Israel, for the LORD Himself was their inheritance. When one of the other tribes was taken into captivity, he had to leave his inheritance behind; but the godly Levite was as rich in Babylon as in

Palestine: death itself could not rob him of his portion. Happy indeed are they who share the Levite's lot! When the LORD JESUS comes again, those, surely, who have stored most in heaven, and have least to leave behind on earth, will render their account with the greatest joy.

"To every man according to his service." The LORD did not say, divide it equally among the families of Levi. There were six wagons, and three families of Levites; but four wagons were given to Merari, two to Gershon, "but unto the sons of Kohath he gave none." At first sight this division appears unfair; but it was and still is the LORD'S plan to give "to every man according to his service." It fell to the lot of Merari to carry the heaviest materials of the tabernacle; the boards, the bars, and the pillars with their heavy sockets of solid silver,E and all the instruments; the pillars of the court, likewise, with their brazen sockets and pins, and their cords,—these formed Merari's weighty burden.

The duty of Gershon was to convey the curtains, hangings, coverings and cords of the tabernacle, and the hangings of the court; for this service, two wagons were as sufficient help as the four were for Merari.

But what of Kohath? His burdens were not light: the ark, with its covering the mercy-seat, and the cherubim of gold overshadowing it, the table and the candlestick, the altars and the vessels of the sanctuary, and all their coverings, these were entrusted to his sons. Heavy they were indeed, but no help had they, "because the service of the sanctuary belonging unto them was that they should bear upon their shoulders."

Sometimes the children of GOD are tempted to murmur when their service seems heavy and but little help is forthcoming: they may perhaps compare their lot with that of others for whom larger provision has been made. But GOD makes no mistakes; according to their service He divides the help, and those who are called to the holiest service are those who can have least assistance. Such are privileged to carry upon their own shoulders sacred burdens that may not

Separation and Service

be shared with less privileged ones. There was ONE Who trod the winepress alone, and of the people there was none with Him; and one who was very like to his MASTER tells us, "At my first answer no man stood with me, but all men forsook me.... Notwithstanding the LORD stood with me, and strengthened me; that by me the preaching might be fully known, and that all the Gentiles might hear." Those who would be near the MASTER in the glory must here drink the cup of sorrow with Him and be baptized with His baptism.

The burden-bearing of the Levites was not to last for ever: once in the Promised Land that service ceased. Nor will our opportunity of burden-bearing be for long; the glorious appearing of our great GOD and SAVIOUR will soon summons the watchful and waiting ones to meet Him in the air. A million a month in China are dying without GOD; now we may seek to win them; now we may suffer to win them. May none of us lose the opportunity of self-denial and service while it

* Weighing more than one cwt. each: the hundred sockets therefore alone weighing over five tons of pure silver.

THE DEDICATORY OFFERINGS:
VERSES 10, 11.

"And the princes offered for dedicating of the altar in the day that it was anointed.... And the LORD said unto Moses, They shall offer their offering, each prince on his day, for the dedicating of the altar."

The offerings recorded in the early verses of this chapter were given in connection with the setting up of the Tabernacle, and had reference to its transportation. But the offerings now to be considered had reference to the altar, and the sacrifices to be offered thereon. Their number, their character, and their value are full of significance; and the space accorded to their record by GOD shows the Divine estimation of the altar, and of those gifts which pertain to sacrifice to Him.

The altar points us to our incarnate

SAVIOUR, the CHRIST of GOD, and reminds us that *without shedding of blood there is no remission of sin*. The altar sanctified the gift; the fire on the altar first came down from heaven; all fire that did not come from the altar was strange fire, and could only bring death to the offerer when used in worship, as in the case of Nadab and Abihu.

Do we not need to remember this in the present day, when false teachers deny the atoning character of the death of CHRIST, and vainly imagine that GOD can be served with the unhallowed fires of fleshly activity?

THE DISPLAY OF THE GIFTS.

The twelve princes, the representatives of the Israel of GOD, brought their offerings before the altar, and would have left them there: they were all exactly alike, and the gifts might have been speedily accepted, and briefly recorded, if recorded at all. But the LORD said unto Moses, They shall offer their offering, each prince on his day,—or, literally, *one prince a day*, a sentence which is expressed twice in the Original, showing GOD'S regard for order and method in all things which concern His service, and that He graciously receives and remembers the offerings of each of His faithful. Accordingly all the offerings of each of the princes are here registered by the HOLY SPIRIT in GOD'S Book, as an encouragement to Christian liberality in all ages" (*Wordsworth*).

Does it not seem as though the Divine delight in the offering of His servants was so great that He would have His people also to dwell upon them for twelve consecutive days? And not only does He spread them over twelve days, but He spreads them over seventy-seven long verses in this long chapter; first in minute detail, according as much space to the gifts of the last offerer as to those of the first, and then totalling up the aggregate amount, as though He would say, "Behold the love-gifts of my people! How many and how precious the offerings of each, and how great the value of the whole! Note, too, the persons of the offerers, and that all their gifts were for the dedication of the altar, and show their appreciation of the need for, and the blessed privilege of sacrifice!"

As we mentioned in our introductory chapter, it was through this account, read in a time of great spiritual need, that our mind was opened as never before to see GOD'S great heart of love. We seemed to be reminded of the delight often taken by bride and bridegroom in spreading out for inspection the love-gifts of their friends, that as many as possible may share their gratification in them. Several may have sent similar gifts; but each is set out to the best possible advantage, with the name of the giver attached. And while the intrinsic value of each is not lost sight of, it is the loving thought of which it is the expression that is most prized.

Again, we were reminded of the way in which, in our frequent absence from home and children, wifely letters have cheered and interested us, depicting with motherly tenderness the gifts the children had brought her on her birthday, or other occasion, with a fulness of detail that showed alike the pleasure of the writer and her consciousness of the enjoyment with which the account would be read. Does not the full detail of this chapter reveal, in like manner, the love and tenderness of Him whose Book it is, toward each offerer; and bring out what we may reverently call the mother-side of GOD'S character, Who has condescended to say, "As one whom his mother comforteth, so will I comfort you"?

THE PERSON OF THE OFFERER.
verses 12-17

"And he that offered his offering the first day was Nahshon the son of Amminadab, of the tribe of Judah:" etc.

As we read of the offerings of the twelve princes, we note that, valuable as they manifestly are, the offerer whose love prompted the gifts, is made more prominent in the inspired Record. The person of each offerer is brought before us, both as an individual, and in his relationship to the tribe of which he is the

Separation and Service

representative, before any enumeration is made of his gifts; and when the enumeration has been fully given, we are again reminded of the offerer himself. Could the Divine love and satisfaction be more expressively brought out?

With this thought in view, let us read between the lines of the Record:—

And he that offered his offering—for a glad free-will offering it was—on the first day was Nahshon, Nahshon the son of Amminadab, Nahshon the prince of the tribe of Judah; and his offering was one charger—a silver charger, and a weighty one; the weight thereof was a hundred and thirty shekels: one bowl, also of silver, of seventy shekels weight; not the light shekels of commerce, but the weighty shekels of the Sanctuary. Nor were these vessels empty: both of them were full—full of flour, fine flour, and mingled with oil, destined for a meat-offering.

One spoon was the next gift, yet more precious, a spoon of solid gold, of no less than ten shekels weight. It, too, was full—full of incense.

Next were brought one young bullock, one ram, and one lamb of the first year—all for a burnt-offering. Any one of these might have been offered; Nahshon, however, brought them all, and all to be wholly consumed on the altar, for the enjoyment and satisfaction of GOD alone.

But Nahshon was a sinner, and the tribe he represented were sinful men; a sin-offering therefore was not neglected; and in the order of enumeration this is next mentioned, though, as we have said before, it was offered first—one kid of the goats for a sin-offering.

And, lastly, a princely offering for a sacrifice of peace-offerings; two oxen, five rams, five he-goats, five lambs of the first year—sacrifices on which GOD feasted, as it were, together with His people, and in which the sacrificing priest, the offerer and all his friends had their full share.

And this, all this, was the offering of Nahshon, Nahshon the son of Amminadab.

Twelve times is all this detail repeated —a most emphatic evidence that GOD never wearies in noting the service of

Separation and Service

each one of His people. But even this is not all. In the 84th and following verses of this long chapter we read:—

"This was the dedication of the altar, in the day when it was anointed, by the princes of Israel: twelve chargers of silver, twelve silver bowls, twelve spoons of gold. Each charger of silver weighing a hundred and thirty shekels, each bowl seventy: all the silver vessels weighed two thousand and four hundred shekels, after the shekel of the Sanctuary. The golden spoons were twelve, full of incense, weighing twelve shekels apiece, after the shekel of the Sanctuary; all the gold of the spoons was a hundred and twenty shekels.

"All the oxen for the burnt-offering were twelve bullocks, the rams twelve, the lambs of the first year twelve, with their meat-offering; and the kids of the goats for sin-offering twelve. And all the oxen for the sacrifice of the peace-offerings were twenty and four bullocks, the rams sixty, the he-goats sixty, the lambs of the first year sixty.

"This"—*all this*—"was the dedication

of the altar, after that it was anointed."

THE IMPORTANCE OF THE ALTAR.

In this glad summing up of the great aggregate value of the offerings, we not only get a further view of the Divine complacency in the love-gifts of His people, and in the persons of the offerers, but the object of the offerings is also brought into special prominence. As the list of each prince's offerings was preceded and followed by reference to the *person* of the offerer, so the list of totals is preceded and followed by the thought, This was the dedication of the altar in the day when it was anointed.

The importance of the brazen altar can scarcely be exaggerated. The Tabernacle contained many precious things, each typifying most important truths concerning our LORD and His ministry; the ark on which rested the Shekinah, which enshrined the tables of the law, and was covered by the mercy-seat, the table of shew-bread, the candlestick of gold, and the golden altar were all most

Separation and Service

precious; but, apart from the brazen altar, *there was no access to them for guilty man*; without shedding of blood there is no remission of sin. Hence the recognition by the princes of the importance of the altar; and hence the Divine emphasis placed upon those gifts —an emphasis wholly without parallel in the sacred Records. To the godly Israelite the brazen altar typified that which was fulfilled at the Cross, and well may we exclaim: "GOD forbid that I should glory, save in the Cross of our LORD JESUS CHRIST" (Gal. vi. 14).

* * *

Looking back over the two chapters on which we have been dwelling we see in them a marvellous revelation of Divine love—even in Mosaic times. First, an unrestricted invitation to draw near to GOD; woman or man, of any tribe—whosoever will—may come and be wholly separated unto the LORD—but only in GOD'S way. We learn, too, that in such consecration there is no merit on which man may rest, or in which he may boast; we are at best unprofitable servants, accepted only in the BELOVED, complete only in Him. Yet such consecration gives joy to GOD, and opens the way to wonderful revelations of blessing; blessing which when enjoyed constrains to service, to gift, to recognition of the preciousness of the Altar, of the Cross—a service in which GOD Himself finds delight, and on which He never wearies to dwell.

May GOD make our meditations very practical; and may we "thus judge, that if ONE died for all, then were all dead; and that He died for all, that they which live should not henceforth live unto themselves, but unto Him which died for them and rose again,"—or, as we may better read it, "unto Him which died and rose again for them."

Are we really thus living? GOD knows: eternity will show: what answer does conscience give now? What conclusions do our brothers, sisters, children, friends draw from our lives? Our true self-denial, self-emptying, and giving for CHRIST'S cause practically show *our* real estimate of the value of the Cross of Christ, our real love for the Christ who was crucified for us.

www.ingramcontent.com/pod-product-compliance
Lightning Source LLC
Chambersburg PA
CBHW060340080526
44584CB00013B/855